Robert Doisneau

Robert Doisneau

Three Seconds of Eternity

101 photographs
with an essay by the photographer

te Neues Publishing Company

New York

Published in the U.S.A. and Canada by te Neues Publishing Company, New York

Translated from the French by John M. King

Cover illustrations:
Front cover: *The kiss in front of the Hôtel de Ville*, 1950
Back cover: *The Accordionist, rue Mouffetard*, 1951

First published 1979 by Contrejour, Paris, under the title *Trois secondes d'éternité*
© 1983/1997 by Schirmer/Mosel, Munich
© for the photographs by Robert Doisneau/Rapho 1997

Typeset by Typograph, Munich
Offset lithography by Nova Concept, Berlin in Novatone®
Printed and bound by EBS, Verona

ISBN 3-8238-2124-5

Three Seconds of Eternity

Robert Doisneau

The Golden Lion

You'll no doubt be very glad to hear that I can't do a thing before my morning coffee.

In this damn hotel, wanting a cup coffee at eight o'clock in the morning is a sign of mental instability. That's our good old French hotel tradition for you; I begin to understand all those caravans buzzing about on our roads – their owners cover thousands of miles looking for the 'café negro' or the 'café solo' or the 'capuccino' they can't get on French soil.

I pace round in the entrance hall; in vain I shuffle my feet, clear my throat, shift the chairs – not only does no one come, but there is not even the slightest gurgle in the plumbing that might give me some hope of seeing someone of authority behind the coffee-machine.

The sight of the goldfish swimming mockingly round in its bowl and the smell of stale tobacco smoke drive me out on to the terrace.

I had arrived the day before in the middle of the local festival. Now, as the flags droop, it's difficult to imagine the effervescence of the population in this little square, in the middle of which there remains the musicians' dais.

It would be more accurate to use the word 'scaffold' to describe the place where the season's hits were executed without mercy. It's not that they deserved a better fate, that's not the point, but that dais was twenty yards from my bed, and that's an important detail. Who, I ask you, would not be in a fusty humour under such circumstances?

I must have slept a bit, though, because I failed to notice the explosion and its atomic mushroom cloud, which have apparently annihilated the little town.

Footsteps. A man emerges from the other side of the square, a survivor like myself, but brisk and lively. It's a Japanese, taking his Nikon for a walk. To keep up that pace he must have had two or perhaps three cups of tea, lucky devil.

Just look at him: he sets off, aims . . . click! turns, steps back . . . click! He sees me, and here he comes straight towards me. Five yards away he stops. And smiles; his incisors and canine teeth are gold – I nearly said 'and so am I', but no, I'm petrified. Click! He's got me in his box. In the time it takes me to recover, the Japanese disappears behind the twelfth-century church.

He's just about finished me off. To get up so early after a sleepless night, only to fall prey to a voracious Japanese – my horoscope can't be all that good.

The bright light which has climbed on to the roofs begins to descend along the façades. To each chimney, dormer and gutter, the sun offers the luxury of a personal shadow. These masterly lighting effects construct a bright vision of the little town in its lethargy, dismantle it into a thousand pieces and give us a child's view of it.

Children's drawings do indeed show such perceptions, drawn with acute curiosity. For them the game consists in rearranging the sum of received emotions on the surface of the paper, without bothering too much about logic. The morning sun, underlining everything, is an invitation to storytelling, and by sharpening our curiosity it brings us hopes of new discoveries.

The role of the morning sun – look how excellently things are organised – is to reawaken that inexplicable feeling, optimism. Cock-a-doodle-doo!...

Not all mornings are so brassy, so sprinkled with confetti. In Paris we're used to a diffuse light in which trees, houses, monuments with their blurred details, appear as if modelled all in one. That's because of the greyish awning which the famous sky of the Ile-de-France starts to spread over the town from dawn, just as one puts a cover on valuable furniture.

The light oozing through this awning, coming from a large number of different points, lights up all facets of the view in a uniform way.

Depending on their orientation, the buildings have more or less brilliance, but no part of them is really in the shade. The resulting absence of mystery leads to an analytical way of seeing, somewhat cold and completely devoid of poetry. Without the reference point of the wandering shadows, time seems to crawl.

That is when passive contemplation comes into its own, when with a touch of lassitude, one observes things with what it is appropriate to call the 'wisdom of age'. And from there it is but a short step to saying that this veiled light is the light of wise men. In any case, real old wise men have so little to say about such things that they stretch what they have to say by saying 'Well, there you are . . . there you are, then . . .', and here comes a coffee pot carried by a dishevelled girl, a living proof that a chambermaid is not necessarily trim.

Is it really essential to get up early to confront mankind with this elementary principle, that any feeling body immersed in light of a given quality receives an impulse to its mood consonant with the quality of that light?

This morning's light clearly gives me a feeling of well-being. Thoughtlessly I say 'It's a beautiful time of day', offering my smug gratitude to a notion of time – something totally insensible. Time has no use for my compliments – it can be neither beautiful nor ugly; its gluttony makes one dizzy. The only way of dealing with it is using the system so beloved of anarchists – individual repetition. The attempt's doomed to failure, of course; let's pretend it isn't, though, for the sake of the gesture.

The most beautiful gesture of all, and the simplest, is the spontaneous reflex with which one tries to hold on to a moment of happiness which is about to vanish. Or there is the more calculated gesture, that of seizing an image from the passage of time and brandishing it as a proof of the existence of one's own universe. Or a gesture may be motivated by aesthetic considerations – then we say that the composition is harmonious because the various wandering elements combine spontaneously and fleetingly into the familiar shape of a letter of the alphabet. This artistic refinement seems to me to be similar to a conditioned reflex.

For a long time I used to think it was vital to apply one's entire energy towards cutting the ham of time into thinner and thinner slices. The results are disappointing; if the slice is not streaky with a bit of past and a hint of future, nothing remains on the transparency but gesticulations devoid of taste.

André Hardellet has written disturbing things about that, comparing the present to a fine ray of light which moves along events that remain immobile. For him, for one who chooses to stand still, the game consists in fixing experience and thus enlarging the ray to make it into a docile instrument for contemplating time.

If one messes around with time, not all the slices of ham or rays of light called to one's aid will ever be able to defend one totally from a vague anguish. So, in his panic, the poor photographer can find no better magic formula in his limited vocabulary than the traditional 'Don't move! No movement, please!'

Now my coffee is completely cold.

Breathless memories

Lapses of memory are an excellent excuse used by old men to put their forged coinage into circulation. Chaos in the drawers of memory is not unintentional. As if by chance those memories which give us no excuse for self-congratulation have gone astray, while those which allow us to compliment our egos remain bobbing on the surface. If some drivelling ancestor declares slyly: 'The opposite of what I say is not necessarily true', he disarms possible opponents and avoids risks. But that does not concern us. First of all, I'm not an old man – it was only by sheer carelessness that I crossed the threshold of ripe maturity, and secondly there remain the images which restrain, like barriers, any attempt to go astray.

There's no doubt about it, I was made to be the lord of a castle. I can just see myself, strolling in the avenues of my park with my tutor, whose sole concern is to make the transfusion of knowledge painless. Fate has decreed otherwise; in the absence of a castle I've been compelled to make my own way in the world, where I have found my niche as a photographer. In other words, I have had to earn my living doing photographic work, all kinds of work, not always elevating.

From Billancourt to Venice, from the Renault works to the Bestegui ball. No danger of getting stale with routine.

Regrets? Yes, some. Doing work like that all the time prevents one from keeping a weather eye open for better opportunities. All those hours upon hours in the laboratory, which take so much energy, are a good training in patience, but carry the risk of causing one to give up in resignation.

It seems that total freedom is not desirable, and that the best resolutions only bear fruit under restraint. So I have had my fair share, and should thank the Almighty for not making me the heir to a castle.

The gently yellowing pictures remind me of the many hobby-horses I've ridden in my time. In chronological order I wanted: to faithfully reproduce the epidermis of objects;

to discover the hidden treasures we tread on every day; to cut time into fine slices; to fraternise with phenomena; to find out what makes certain pictures attractive. The rest of the cavalry disappears in the fog.

This way of presenting things, as if they were a scheme of entertainment for an aesthete, risks obscuring the crushing situation I was in – the need to exchange my pictures for the essentials of life. I often lost the threads of this programme of mine – it was so inextricably interwoven with my material needs, cutting across the happy or sad events of an epoch.

It may seem scanty to you, but it can occupy a whole life.

Nowadays it's not a disgrace to be a photographer – there are even some who've married princesses. When I started, a photographer was at best an ingenious potterer whose activity was tolerated provided he kept well within the limits of established organisations. As for the Gentlemen of Official Culture, they did not mess around – at the mere word 'photography' you could see them ditch their old private quarrels and close ranks in solidarity.

Even my aunt Zoë, who used to say 'Do you play the pianoforte?' introduced me by saying 'This is my little nephew the designer, that is my nephew who does studies in engraving'.

But photographer, oh no! By walking the streets and associating with riffraff, the poor angel had gone to the bad. And as regards engraving, my aunt wasn't lying completely. I had studied lithography (if you can call it studying) at the Ecole Estienne. The idea was to squeeze the largest number of shading-lines into the minimum amount of space with the aid of a line-counter. After a certain number of days, which seemed never-ending, you had produced a scroll of foliage incorporating an angel, an allegorical figure or the arms of the town of Nancy.

The professors – grey overalls, watch-chains, black felt hats – congregated between two studios to discuss the latest scandal, Van Dongen at the Salon d'Automne. 'He doesn't give a damn for the world – green eyelashes! Neither flesh nor fowl; my six-year-old kid can do just the same. Dagnan-Bouveret! The reflection of the umbrella on the floor! Now Meissonier, he wipes the floor with the lot of them.'

It took a full four years of technical training and cultural baths to get, at long last, a diploma.

The diploma really amused people outside, where that antiquated technique was no longer practised except by a few craftsmen in the Marais. And those acrobats of the needle and the graving-tool worked at a breathtaking speed, being in such a hurry to get off to watch the horse-racing.

It was a mare that helped me to turn the corner. It was called Urania and was unbeatable. As a mere formality, I had handed over a week's wages – for drawing a Bordeaux wine label – to the little greenish man in the rue Saint-Claude.

A wine label's not a big thing, but I had still managed to fit in, in English copperplate above the name of the chateau, a general view of the cellars and the medals won in the exhibition of 1889.

In making the label I had benefited from the experience of an old hand – the same one who had given me the tip about Urania. And a miracle happened: on the day of the race Urania affected a slight migraine and stayed well down in the field. I definitely seemed to be collecting bad advice!

My professional training seemed a farce; I felt that the whole of that mummified instruction was utterly worthless. For four years I had only left my lithographic stone to go and screw up my eyes in front of Graeco-Roman plaster-casts, measuring the proportions with a piece of charcoal held at arm's length. At the same time, and it caused me much confusion, a voice whispered in my ear: 'Never slavishly copy Nature, otherwise photographs and casts would be works of art too.'

The 'in' word at the time was 'stylisation'. In decorative composition it was essential to 'stylise' – that was vague enough to lead to angular, symmetrical representations bathed in tones of sepia, black and gold.

All that poisonous old rubbish had to be chucked out of the window. That old teaching system, which was a complete cul-de-sac, had to be turned round; the new method couldn't fail to set me on the right road. That was unbeatable logic, with the added spice of disobedience.

I'd have given the whole gamut of Roman emperors for the chestnut-seller in the Place d'Italie. No professor would have taken the slightest notice of that little man from the Auvergne, who might be ill-shaven, but who possessed in my eyes the advantage of being a real living man of flesh and blood.

I joined the vengeful opposition, and decided that the concern which had animated artists for centuries had been exactitude. Not only was I going to copy; I was going to do it with total devotion and the greatest possible fidelity. And more: to make the divorce yet more complete, I was going to make my experiment in the heart of a disregarded world using a despised means of expression – photography! That'd show them!

So, with a heavy heart, I plunged into an empirical apprenticeship. That begins by reading the instructions in the boxes of photographic plates. From then on, the Lumière agenda illuminated my steps.

I read more and more technical texts. If one discounts page 242 of L. P. Clerc's book on the relations of tobacco with the photographer – here's a sample: 'The use of pipes with lids, which has been recommended to smoking photographers, can be considered superfluous' – one need not be ashamed to say that all that literature is pretty grim.

Impelled by the desire to tame the opportunities of optical chemistry in order to command its favours, I became the keen, but sole, student of my own further education centre. 'Sensitometry' – for me, the word was explosive in its novelty. There it was in black and white: 'It is impossible for any photographer worth his salt to ignore sensitometry.' So as not to die an ignoramus, I took the book's advice and acquired a Filmograph.

With its eyepiece and rheostats, the black-painted thing had an air of scientific gravity. The moment I sat down before it, I remembered the engraving that hangs in all elementary schools – Louis Pasteur in his laboratory. That example gave me courage, so here goes: horizontally the decimal logarithms of exposure – good! Vertically the optical densities, right! One had only to join the dots with a line to obtain the characteristic curve of the emulsion under study.

Alas! from one sheet of squared paper to another, the curves were different. The instructions said nothing about such a case. There was a fault somewhere, or perhaps, in our age of intense specialisation, I was not made for scientific research. It was the phrase of Pagnol's César – 'Now, my boy, let the others do a bit of measuring' – which saved me from my humiliation. So we parted: the Filmograph ended up in the cellar and I turned to practical work.

In the end, a few quite passable shots of materials that the hand likes to touch – cloth, seashells, feathers, porcelain, a whole gallimaufry of docile subjects – gave me the confidence to put my talents to the test.

At last I was able to capture the noble subject of a gas lamp. That gas lamp was the first flower of a whole bouquet composed entirely of town furniture. Piles of paving-stones, railings round trees, builder's lamps, manhole covers – my nosegay filled me with pleasure.

Even today, I find nothing ridiculous in my delight. Having been an engraver, I saw everything through a magnifying-glass – much the best tool for discovering the nobility of those objects, with their patina of time and age. I was alone in that view – at first people did not look; they passed by exhausted, chewing over their court cases about party walls, which I overheard in their conversations.

I felt at the same time misunderstood and highly distinguished; I would never have dared, however, to raise my camera under their noses. With an innocent air, mildly, I directed two laser-beams at them and projected on their brand-new retinas (the best sensitive surface ever invented) a fragment of that caricature of humanity. Fortunately, my timidity stopped me from going into action and forced me to await a less aggressive phase. One must be fair. Some adults who seem to have retained a sufficiently intact critical sense have shown me that timidity can be overcome.

And they, on election nights, came and threw stones at my uncle's window-shutters – even in my circles they weren't thought much of. People called them 'hooligans in caps'. As such, the police didn't spare them. The posters they put up illicitly were not perhaps in the best taste, but I secretly admired their audacity and their team spirit. They seemed to be the only ones who really wanted to change the idiotic scenery that was in front of my eyes all the time.

The macramé curtains, the felt slippers, the pot-covers and the furniture covers were for the chop – that was certainly in their programme, which at the same time no doubt made a clean sweep of the whole litany of good principles: the savings-book, hair well behind the ears, saluting the flag, being a good son, a good father, a good citizen, and ending up with the long service medal. As for those who followed those precepts, I saw them all round me, with their hangdog look – they were as boring as the rain.

I was desperate to leave those seedy, shabby individuals to their own devices, to set off – where to, I had no clear idea. To anything that was so beautiful that it took your breath away. Anything at all – music, poetry, faith in anything. I felt a desire for luxury articles. Such things, of no immediate use, were absent from the local shops.

In the surroundings I had grown up in, it was the done thing to be content with surrogates. For those ordinary people everything had to be cut down a bit, had to be vaguely showy and not cost too much. All was imitation leather or imitation wood. Scallops to make garden borders, barred bedsteads transformed into rabbit-hutches, marrow-bones into key-fobs.

Everything was re-used, the poets just the same as the rest. Great works of poetry were used as mere memory-training. A laborious task that took a great deal of blood and sweat – hence the term 'bloody poets' used by the pupils.

The poets in their turn were expected to do their duty in civic studies lessons. Victor Hugo was the teachers' favourite for this purpose.

I was in the choir the day the war memorial was inaugurated. Victor Hugo had provided the words; the music was by Monsieur Levif, our singing teacher. A choir in three voices at least. 'Those who gave their lives that we may li – ive, for them we at their grave shall gri – ieve . . .' All the schoolchildren were there, both boys and girls. Judging by the cacophony, there had been no rehearsals, but it was good fun all the same.

We all came together again at the final chord. Then the veil fell, disclosing a bronze widow showing her son a name on a marble plaque. The monument was by Monsieur Vasseur, whose father was on the town council.

That morning remained a powerful memory for me – that wasn't the kind of poetry I was yearning for. Nor was mystical ecstasy – there was a crack somewhere.

The priest of St Saturnin's church seemed to me at first to be a sort of super-astronomer. When he talked about the Almighty and the Infinite, you could only see the whites of his eyes. In general he presented things in a much more attractive way than worldly maths problems with water-taps. Little by little his magic gestures enveloped me in a sky-blue cocoon, and it felt good. A St-Sulpice-like sweetness transported me far above the zinc roofs of my suburb.

One detail spoilt all that. In the course of one of these transports I reached the height of two inscriptions. One said 'God sees everything'; the other, 'God does not like naughty children'.

They were in the handwriting of our teacher – with modestly lowered eyes, she was telling us wonderful stories about our great-great-grandparents. Judging by what she said, the Heavenly Father had nothing better to do than conduct inspections of tiny tots. To be concerned about the sex of angels shows a meddlesome spirit, unworthy of a Heavenly Father who was infinitely good and infinitely kind.

At a stroke, I had become profoundly distrustful. The priest was a good deal too violent when he was playing tag-ball – and that motorbike rearview mirror he'd mounted on the side of the tabernacle, was it to keep an eye on his flock or to control his ecstasies? The spell was broken. I shall never know the unalloyed pleasure of bawling hymns under Gothic vaults. I was destined to forget the putrefying smell of his breath.

But for those details I might today be an unconditional integrationist.

Let us not wallow in regrets; let us return to photography.

It is difficult to escape from one's childhood memories. You know how it is: one word leads to another, and all of a sudden you've gone right off the subject. Where were we before that digression? Ah yes, we were talking about passing figures and timidity.

The same train of thought which took the first film-makers towards the first gesticulations in front of the camera brought me to the conviction that the caricature of humanity that I saw so clearly offered the photographer the best models he could wish for. I know a fish-pond beside the Saint-Ouen gate that was swarming with ideal extras for a pirate film. I had only to go and help myself.

Cheerfully I set up my tripod and screwed a wooden camera on to it. Putting one's head under a black cloth does not necessarily make one invisible. I learnt that simple fact when, having finished aiming, I returned into the light of day. All the gamblers were watching me, frozen immobile as if for a portrait photo. Someone said 'Stop it, Paulo!' Paulo came towards me; there was an odour of misunderstanding in the air.

I know it now; in front of his normal public Paulo would have done a circus trick, in which I would have been the vaulter. Paulo must have judged that I was not up to it, but despite his respect for sportsmanship he expressed himself crudely. I don't remember the exact words, but broadly speaking he said he had never seen such a bugger, that I would do better to go and play in my yard, and a lot more things of less importance.

I moved my equipment a bit further away. As a beginning, it was not an unqualified success.

Seen from close to, reality was rougher than expected. Coming to terms with it required an apprenticeship. On three or four Sundays I wielded my black cloth without a hitch. The result was published in *Excelsior*, on the very last page.

I could just see myself on the *Petit Parisien* poster, dressed in knickerbockers, one foot on a globe of the world: Reporter.

Underneath the suburb where I grew up flows the Bièvre, now taken over by the Sewage Department. Yesterday, rather more than half a century ago, at the outlet from the tanning works, one could see a brownish liquid trickling out, which did not smell good. That was the Bièvre.

Down in the town, the walls, riddled with saltpetre, enabled one to draw nice graffiti with one's finger in their soft plaster. The streets beside the church were crooked, full of nooks and crannies from which projected much anarchic plumbing. Above the roofs rose, like watchtowers, lattice-work, drying racks with skins hanging from them. On the heights towards Montrouge perched the little pavilion with its awning over the steps and railings repainted every spring.

As for green spaces, one couldn't complain, with the market gardens and the scent of fresh celery, and the grey-green spaces of waste land, not yet called play areas – the expression had not yet been invented. Naturally it was urgent to organise this muddle, to transform it into a functional tool. Ladies and gentlemen, it is done, it's respectable, and it's ugly.

Formerly, that absurd setting at least had the merit of imparting a sense of worth to the people who walked about in it. Not the old people; they had faded gradually into the landscape in a kind of mimicry, but the young – it took quite some nerve to return from the forest of Sénart on bicycles covered with daffodils and plunge into this greyness. Once again, the girls were the most insolent, flowers in all this slag, promenading their brand-new little breasts in the sinister rue Frileuse. Pretty shepherdesses of Gentilly who go to Robinson's on Sunday to dance the tango with salesman princes from the Samar. People really didn't deserve to have eyes – no one looked at them in all their beauty.

Then Zorro appeared, armed with a camera straight from the suburbs of Brunswick (Germany) – the Rolleiflex.

As a weekend photographer, or in between times, I tried to capture this absurd scenery and to mix among its cast of characters. Gradually I collected pictures; some I quite liked, but I felt very alone – my photos of this banal suburb aroused no interest whatever in my circle, because of course I was addressing suburban people.

I was still nagged by doubt – was I perhaps completely mad? I needed authoritative advice. At that time there lived a great lady of photography. Her success, the deference she was accorded, allowed her the luxury of benevolence. Summoning all my courage, I asked for an appointment.

I remember her flat, rather over-full to my taste, encrusted with green plants, busts, and heavy trimmings, giving an atmosphere at the same time solemn and very plush. I began by sitting down on an open book; there was an awkward moment, then I unpacked my works. On the velvet of the divan, my 18 x 24 prints spread out in all their insolent poverty.

Just as one lights a perfume-burner to dispel bad smells, the lady hastened to show me how it should be done. She left me alone for a moment – I took the opportunity to collect up my absurdities. She returned beaming, with an armful of very large pictures. What struck me at once was the generous margins, but also the confidence of the signature and the velvetiness of the mount. I can't quite remember what was in the pictures, but it was something in the picturesque line. I went out backwards, bowing politely.

Seeing what I'm like, that visit brought me the greatest possible consolation; hardly had I closed the door than I knew I was on the right track.

To give me a view of life inside the humming factories which stood everywhere in that part of the town, Providence opened the doors of the best one to me. The Renault factory in Billancourt.

I was commissioned to take industrial photographs. To the great satisfaction of my bosses, I rapidly learnt the tricks of taking a good portrait of a Cazenave lathe or a Cincinnati milling machine. There was no question of taking the pictures other than with an 18 x 24 camera, which with a suitable tripod, spare bodies, and the essential odds and ends, constituted a load of some twenty kilos. Thus encumbered, I walked through the streets and workshops, thinking of the advertising slogan that was the basis of all their publicity: the Renault factories cover an area equal to that of the city of Chartres. And my God, that was quite possible.

I have happy memories of some diversions which occasionally upset the daily routine and allowed me to leave the factory with impunity. Sometimes there was a visit by a petrol king – it was in front of the Hôtel Crillon, around the wonderful Reinastella, in the crush, that I made my first contacts with accredited reporters. Eight passengers sitting comfortably facing the road, all cleared for action, we went to the Park of St-Cloud in a Vivastella full of the slimmest typists of the postal service.

I've left the best thing till last – the parade of elegance in the Bois de Boulogne in June – the Vivasport convertibles, the dream creatures wearing sun-bonnets which flew off with every acceleration, the white greyhounds, the president of the jury, Monsieur André de Fouquières, who welcomed them with 'Ah, here's Beauty and the Beast', and 'I kiss your hand', and 'We've met before…'

A whole world of beautiful people, carefree, who need only raise their heads to see the smoke of Billancourt. After that short excursion into cloud-cuckoo-land, some workshops seemed to me even more awful: the steelworks, the paint shop, the tyre shop, the heat-treatment shop. It was common to meet a tyrant in a white overall whose yelling and shouting made life there even worse. During the strikes of 1936 the one who reigned on the Ile Seguin was thrown into the Seine a dozen times. In effigy, of course.

The magnesium flashlights were a diversion for a whole workshop. A 50-gram flash exploded – boom! – and fifty workmen were hilarious. The little photographer's good deed. Don't imagine it was just a short episode – I played my part for five years. I'm good at taking forty winks in the early-morning bus among my workmates.

A dream came true: 'You're wanted in Reception.' And there was the man of Providence, and he said: 'I've heard about your colour photographs on paper – wonderful, simply wonderful. Come at once, my chauffeur's waiting for you.'

Indeed, for months, in our kitchen in the evenings, I had been perfecting a photographic printing process, preparing my escape.

Today, I don't mind giving you the recipe. First make exposures of the subject in three colours. With the negatives thus obtained, expose three gelatines previously tinted in primary colours and enriched with bichromate. Make sure you get it right: the gelatines have to be stripped in a lukewarm solution of bleaching-water and sawdust, then transferred to celluloid sheets coated with beeswax and petroleum solution. It is enough to treat the three images as if peeling a transfer, and, taking the greatest possible care in adjusting them, to place them in the order yellow-red-blue on the final backing. The most one can say is that the finished picture will not be a slavish copy of the world.

Today I have only one single picture created in my kitchen laboratory. I think people with severely impaired vision see the world like that. I have given you this wearisome description in an attempt to show you the depth of my yearning for freedom.

At long last, someone took notice of my profound aspirations. He showed me the door with the following reason: repeated lateness. It was the head of the personnel department. I found myself out in the street, where there

was so much to see, with great joy and yet with a vague apprehension. Five years of factory dull one's initiative. Dulled or not, the needs of life forced me to make another start.

It's funny how after any bid for freedom there's always some sinister obstacle in the background preparing its bludgeon. That's how it was in early summer 1939. My desire to share my enthusiasm with others was destined not to find the most favourable climate for several seasons. I had to shelve my strivings towards the light of inspiration – rigged out in soldier's puttees, the only light I was going to see was the light infantry.

From that moment on, I had to devote all my efforts to preserving my unique way of seeing, which the top brass seemed to take precious little notice of. Even if they had known, I don't think it would have changed anything; the hour of sentimentality had not struck. But I found their arguments weak: you can't make an omelette without breaking eggs, you know what they could do, those lads in berets, a smart battalion, spurs dead straight, the illustrious names under the sacred vault. He said all that, our colonel, to make us become career soldiers. He was offering us a sort of refresher course.

It's important to keep an overview of one's experiences, but perhaps because of my apprenticeship with the magnifying glass, my memory only projects tiny fragments – in such detail, however, that I have to take care not to let my anecdotes run away with me.

It's just about excusable to arouse memories, but those little shits who stroll around with the most awful military cast-offs and the most evil insignia, they don't know, those poor innocent little lambs with a rosette from Villette, that to make them look really sweet they need a block warden's whistle, a blue lantern, a ration card for J3, an interzone pass, a yellow star, a red placard and the instructions for using a wet stone and a pen. All that stuff exudes a sticky sadness which I find unwarranted in civilian clothes.

On the wartime black market vegetables were impossibly expensive, but curiously men's lives were cheap. At best, when people emerged at the end having lost no more than a few years of their youth, they thought they'd been lucky. They were so amazed to find themselves still alive that they went a bit mad. You saw some of them going down into the cellar saying they were going dancing.

Printers were in no better state, and tended towards the frenetic – like addicts suffering withdrawal symptoms, they wanted illustrations, quick, no matter what, no matter how. This atmosphere led to a visual world of very bad taste but basically healthy, created with such verve that every time I find a piece of printing dating from that time I find it impossible to feel any remorse. After the darkness came the storm – it's certainly not easy to keep to one's resolutions.

But what resolutions exactly? A letter helped to refresh my memory; the writing was angular, almost fractured, and it said: '... as to your photos of the suburbs and their people, I'm completely carried away.' I had never dared to hope for such a compliment. It was the only one, but it came from Blaise Cendrars.

I had met him at the barber's in Aix-en-Provence; from under the shaving-foam he talked about Gilles de Rais to the barber, who stood with his razor arrested in mid-air.

We went to his place in the rue Georges Clémenceau. He gave me some rum to drink in a big glass, which gives those who aren't used to it a strong impression of warmth. He recounted a walking-tour round Paris with Fernand Léger between Villejuif and Arcueil, in the course of which Fernand Léger had been beaten up by a troop of gypsies. In that jungle, my God, that was quite possible. I knew what the area looked like from having taken photos there, and that shook me out of my torpor – it's amazing to be in Aix-en-Provence, talking in lyrical terms of Villejuif – usually it's the other way round.

I promised to send him some pictures. 'You'll see the place hasn't changed – honestly, I swear it!' – 'Hey, no, that's the cupboard, the door's here!' and boom!... I went off and slept under an olive tree.

Overjoyed to have found an accomplice of such quality, as soon as I got home I sent him everything I had gleaned from the slopes above the Bièvre. And I had that glowing letter! And he was looking for a publisher! And he was extending to me, as he used to put it, the hand of friendship!

Blaise Cendrars has always been good to me. Coming as I do from Beauce, he insisted on seeing in me a descendant of one of the builders of Chartres, which is pretty damn flattering. Go and check his sources, why be modest, perhaps he was right. The book was published. Autograph session at Delattre's, rue de la Pompe, not without ceremony. A distinguished public. Some book lovers came with armfuls of original editions from their collection, to wring a signature out of Blaise. Not bad profits.

But it was still a depressing evening. As regards the print run, the success was modest: only one edition. That was in

1949 – thirty years later, using the method which involves putting a stick under a cupboard to recover an old cuff-link, galleries, libraries and museums have asked me for illustrations taken from that book.

But in this case, as you see, it would be an exaggeration to talk of a resounding success.

Lemon-squeezer

Nowadays, to become a press photographer is comparatively simple. Having touched Uncle and Aunt for the wherewithal to purchase the equipment, it's enough to push a door which is half open anyway. To live on it is another matter.

In the olden days, the entrance to the profession was defended by traditional dragons which gave intruders a hard time. Those who bore the title wore an armband on which the embroidered legend 'Press' bore witness to their membership of a secret society of which they were the visible initiates. They were the periscope of a gigantic submarine.

'You have never made the Press, therefore you cannot join the Press . . .' The argument was unanswerable, and the physical presence of the group made it final. Whether it was on the steps of the Elysée palace or before the flame of the Unknown Soldier, the group was indeed hermetically sealed, and the material employed imposed a discipline comparable to that required for the smooth operation of an execution squad. To become a member you needed a multicoloured concertina of official passes, badges, permits, and other cards, stamped, countersigned, obtained God knows how.

So much for contents of the pocket. As for the head, it had to contain an archive of clichés that had shown their worth in the past, a collection of props to be used as occasion demanded. For example, the only correct illustration for the women's Paris-Saint-Raphael car rally was a lady touching up her lipstick using the outside rearview mirror of her sports car. It had to be that picture and no other.

Another old favourite: on 25 November it was advisable to capture a little Catherine, drag her to the rue de Cléry, take a bar-stool from the bistro opposite the statue of St Catherine (they were used to it), and get the girl to stand on it, whereupon she starts to giggle and offers the statue a bouquet bought in advance.

The flower of all these traditions was the lily-of-the-valley on the first of May. The crowning glory, the be-all-and-end-all of the profession, and my favourite: the market porters of the Halles offering the President of the Republic the lilies-of-the-valley on the first of May.

Oh, those gallant men in their leather hats! The understanding between market porters and the press photographers is no coincidence – in both professions you find the same group spirit and the same pride in practising a profession of deserved distinction.

Used to finding themselves together with the VIPs on the other side of the barriers that keep the crowd back, press photographers tended to identify themselves with the notables and practise an unconscious elitism, naturally with a hint of contempt for the masses. This familiarity could on occasion push them so far (in the thick of the action and thus excusably of course) as to call distinguished personages by their first names. But that did not happen often.

The journalists treated the photographers with the condescension a staff officer would feel for a mere infantryman. A benevolent condescension, but still it was the journalists who spread those delightful stories in which the press photographers were the fall-guys.

They're often called the infantry of information, and that's not such a bad description. Rain or shine, wind or snow, they were outside with their boxes of tools. Apart from that, they were not overloaded with technical equipment. In any case, in those days people didn't say 'technique' but 'knack'. And indeed you had to be quite handy to manage those monstrosities with their front halves made of guaranteed extra-dry wood, compensated for by a back half made of pure nickel enclosing a magazine with a magic drawer, an excellent tool for manufacturing broken glass. Distance and exposure measured by rule of thumb. The correct use of such a machine ought to have deserved a diploma – it reached the limit of attainable skill.

Today's thinking cameras obviate the need for any apprenticeship and deliver good pictures without visible effort. It takes a lot more to astonish people nowadays.

To deliver an original view of the world, the most important thing is now to conquer the right observation post. The ascent to such a perch can be effected with a variety of methods: by a certain lifestyle, by having useful connections, or of course thanks to a privileged social position.

Let's suppose – it's an unlikely hypothesis, but let's suppose all the same – that at an international meeting the President of the Republic takes a successful series of portraits of his partners. The result would be a world-beater, an unbelievable scoop that all magazines would fight over. And let's suppose that the other heads of state, possessed by the desire to emulate this feat, transformed super-summits into photo-safaris – might that not improve the state of the world?

But we've got off the subject of the intrepid pioneers of reporting.

I fear I've made too much of the complacency of our predecessors when in action; one could say the same about all ages and all coteries. I owe them some compensation by paying homage to the patience with which they endured the most uncomfortable situations.

It must be said that taken individually they were happy to give advice: 'Look lad, in this filthy weather you keep your head well down and you keep your brakes on . . .', which interpreted means: aperture f/8 and slow the shutter-slit down by keeping your thumb on the control button.

When they came out of the magazine, the plates were treated roughly. The prints, which were often taken while the plates were still wet, went if possible to the retouching studio, whence they emerged with the blacks hardened and the whites heightened, with the plastery look of cashiers at the zoo. And when they came off the printing presses, the pictures scattered about in the text looked nice, like currants in a slice of fruit cake.

It all worked like a dream: everyone knew his place and his limits; order reigned.

And then there appeared upon the scene certain iconoclasts who behaved like playful conspirators, some of them from far away – Hungary, it was said. These people claimed to be able to take pictures of Press quality with photographic gadgets that were just about good enough for amateurs. A laughable idea, just preposterous.

And anyway, why worry; when the forces of law and order see that lot arrive, they'll kick them out straight away. And that wasn't such a bad scheme anyway; at official occasions the presence of reporters carrying large cameras was a stamp of approval demonstrating the importance of the event and added a touch of dynamism to the general decorum. As expected, the trouble-makers let themselves be kicked out. It's reasonable to suppose that after several failed attempts the following reasoning may have germinated in their minds: these law enforcers who treat us so badly are doing nothing but tyrannically policing events of no importance.

So let's see what happens elsewhere. Let loose in other arenas which seldom received reporters, they returned with an armful of disturbing pictures – an exotic world, all of four stations away by underground.

When the fur begins to fly, one must be ready for anything. And anyway, why not – let's go right ahead with the creation of the M.L.I., the famous Movement for the Liberation of Images, with its motto the refusal to obey the commandment 'Be beautiful and shut up!' Pictures were fed up with playing supporting roles and demanded to be the stars, even claiming a right to modify information.

People have always seen everything before. Funny – the magazine created by Lucien Vogel in 1930 was called *Vu*: 'seen'.

New material, a new team, a freer conception of viewpoints, intense competition between layouters – who or what can be credited with fathering those magazines so full of ingenious ideas? Anyway, it was a real tonic to have been in on the transformation of the illustrated press.

But let's not get carried away; it must be said that that wonderful zest has given way to sluggishness and that a patronising use of press photos has become the norm. Our photo-vignette has become your photo-pleonasm.

Do you realise that today it's still possible to see a friendly scrimmage on the steps of the Elysée? To what purpose? To capture the expression of a face surrounded by television microphone booms.

One might well ask what message is contained in such a photo. Or rather, one should attempt to see in this frenetic activity the survival of a ritual and homage to traditions. The group spirit has become liberal, and that's a very good thing. The clearing up has been done, but the bronze statue has been left on the mantelpiece. It would have been sacrilege to remove it.

Old memories, dried flowers, the nostalgia of rainy days are the companions of old age, but fairy tales projected into the future and reserved for the young are formidable sluts messing about with drugs.

In the press photo the myth of the hero lives on.

In this case the fairy tale suggests to the young that they should run away from the daily grind and follow in the footsteps of Tarzan, Zorro, Tintin and some Formula I drivers. Right at the end the young candidates experience the adventure in which they can exercise their generosity, their courage and their heroism. There are dangers of course, it's a man's game, but oddly, the memory of the

victims, those who did not return, exercises a powerful fascination and dispels the last reservations against becoming the 'Baras' or the 'Vialas' of the 24 x 36. With your sparkling new camera, just you think before deciding to pass the point of no return, my lad.

After epic accounts which make one's spine tingle, how do you intend to describe the alternative with equal lyricism? That alternative consists in sticking with the others and finding a thousand reasons for celebration in a universe that's right here. And it wouldn't be very clever to try and tear you away from the fanfares of adventure by suggesting you might try a little flute solo.

The height of clumsiness is to talk of patience now, and yet there is no other way of learning to win over that lucky chance whose complicity is indispensable. Having patience is not to pay too high a price for the good fortune of being for an instant the astonished witness of an unexpected harmony.

Believe me, it's a pretty rare luxury to be able to put under the nose of our contemporaries, blinded by moving pictures, one of those little treasures which would otherwise have disappeared into the wastepaper-basket of time.

When Jacques Prévert said of Edouard Boubat that he was a great peace correspondent, he was paying him a great compliment.

A ball in a pinball machine

Nowadays I've got the confidence; I go to Paris every day, but I can never get rid of the feeling that I'm only visiting. My suburban childhood won't let me go. Paris – that was the other side of the fortress walls. My nose to the window-pane, I used to watch the yellow tram go past. The 93, Arcueil to Châtelet. On its route across the suburb it was a single-track line with passing places.

I had the good luck to live opposite a set of points. From my window I could watch the conductor get off and, hanging on the rope like a bellringer, attempt to transfer the trolley-pole to the other wire. He never managed it the first time; if he was too clumsy, the passengers used to get off to give him advice and it all ended in a slanging-match. In any case there was always a firework-display of blue sparks, it was fantastic. Oh, we were never bored at home, and sometimes we even took that tram, too. The conductor, seen from close to, had much more authority than seen from my window. 'How old's the little fellow, then?' And he used to call out the stops: Peupliers – Rungis – Glacière . . . and we plunged into the heart of Paris along the boulevard Saint-Michel and pulled up behind the Châtelet theatre on the rails which were borrowed at night by the steam vegetable-wagons of the Arpajonais.

More of that another time, my young readers. Let's leave the number 93 in the transport museum.

So I have no right to the registered trademark of a Parisian and yet I know that town from walking its streets in every direction. Do you know those Japanese steps, those stepping-stones which allow one to cross a lawn without touching it? Paris is a bit like that for me. I can go from Montrouge to the Porte de Clignancourt in a sort of dotted line – I can't cover more than 400 yards without meeting someone I know: the owner of a bistro, a cabinet-maker, a printer, a bookseller, a painter or simply someone I've met in the street and with whom I keep in touch. It holds one up a bit, but it's fun.

I take care to vary my route so as to discover new actors and new settings instead of mechanically steeping myself in familiar charms.

No matter where you look, there's always something brewing. You only have to wait, you have to watch for a long time before the curtain deigns to rise. So I wait, and every time the same high-flown formula trots into my mind: Paris is a theatre in which you pay for your seat with wasted time. And I'm still waiting.

Standing still in the middle of people running in all directions is suspicious behaviour. I found that out one day as I stood there. A stranger whispered in my ear: 'You're on the run – I'm a jailbird too!'

This way of life gives rise to a different vision from other people's. Most people nowadays grope around in the scenery they know, with just an occasional glance so as not to miss their step. The charter-flights are full of people who won't condescend to half-open an eye until they have travelled thousands of kilometres. If they replaced the kilometres by wasted time, they'd be able to attain the same happy state of receptivity.

Just recently, I regret to say, I had to admit the failure of my system. I told you I used to vary my route, well, one day I inevitably ended up in an area of brand-new concrete high-rise blocks, and as usual I waited. Nothing happened. But still, I didn't feel like taking pictures of vertical perspectives or with arty-crafty special effects. Okay, so people are away in the daytime, so let's wait for the evening. The street lights came on, but I still didn't see a soul about.

The inhabitants had slipped into the underground car parks, were sucked up by the lifts and had returned to their televisions without becoming visible.

After the news programmes a few dogs came out and watered the bits of potted green, while their masters, a few paces from the entrance, played casually with their leashes. Apart from that I didn't see anything remarkable at all – that must be the best flop of my career.

The atmosphere of boredom around these dormitory towns is different from that in my home suburb, which is not grey; it's just the opposite, smothered with make-up in garish colours, it tries to disguise itself by assuming a frolicsome aspect. From time to time an impresario is engaged to sprinkle the surroundings with Breton pancake-booths, weaving-looms and fire-eaters, whose job is to bring a touch of the fairground and a bit of proletarian fun. What the Nazi commandant of Greater Paris didn't dare to do in 1944 has been achieved by property speculators without the blast of explosives.

First of all, the good people were politely requested to take their rank smell elsewhere. The operation was carried out with great care. I remember the exhibition in the Hôtel de Ville showing models of the planned refurbishment of the district of les Halles. It was wonderful; the public were admitted, and there were big books for them to make suggestions, which were guaranteed careful attention. At the same time, pest exterminators wandered about the district dressed all in white, carrying buckets of poison, giving Parisians the impression that they had just escaped an outbreak of cholera.

So the street was cleared of strollers, the motorists in their aquariums tapped their foreheads, and on the pavements one encountered only people running to or from underground or mainline stations, always late and often aggressive. Long after the bulldozers had ceased to torment the town, débris continued to accumulate in the form of violent sinister festivals which left the streets full of broken glass in which it was not a good idea to crawl around.

It would take a great deal more to put me off – I'm the very last person to give up my gawping. The very word itself is in retreat, as if one were to say 'My dear fellow, do take a drop of Frontignan before going to the cinematograph in your touring-car!"

Dated or not, if there's only one gawper left alive, it'll be me. Nothing prevents me from going on the pont Alexandre III where the bronze makes bubbles with its crowd of plump women and chubby children, a pretty finde-siècle fantasy, and over there in the background the geometrical arrogance of the Hôtel des Invalides trimmed by a border of rusting cannons and topped by the dome under which Napoleon lies, pinned down at last under tons of red porphyry.

From there I go and rest my elbows on the parapet on the Quai du Louvre opposite Wyers, the angling shop. From here Paris extends as if on a great panoramic screen – to the left the Pont-Neuf with its two Louis XIII houses in the middle, on which Henri IV looks down from his horse, justly proud of the building talents of his youngster. Opposite, down at water level, is the garden of Vert-Galant with its population of long-haired, bearded guitar-strummers – a glance to the right and there is the pont des Arts, once a museum of drawing in chalks, while in the background a tiny Eiffel Tower reminds you pleasantly of its presence.

Pause for a cigarette, then I cross the lock gates at the Quai de la Rapée and take a boat up to la Villette; in the tunnel I look to see if the ventilation shafts let the sunlight in. When we put in at the lock at the Hôtel du Nord – atmosphere, atmosphere – I hesitate between the bakery in the rue Ste-Marthe and the flights of steps in the passage Julien Lacroix, and finally opt for Ménilmontant. Alas! the turret in the rue Vilin has disappeared, and the house of Madame Rayda the fortune-teller, and the elegantly curved gas lamp number 3593.

Even on the heights the speculators have struck. They see to it that Paris does not risk becoming one of those museum cities like bouquets of artificial flowers which lack the charm of transience. I feel biodegradable, so I tend to head for the threatened suburbs. I like districts in which the houses have an individual character; I can only feel happy in streets where you can see at the same time a pensioner with his white dog, a florist, a girl on roller-skates, and a fat man.

To work in the midst of all this teeming life you have to have firm principles and not let yourself be distracted – and I had resolved to find my materials exclusively in daily life, avoiding all picturesqueness. Given a choice between a member of the sect of Gentle Friends of Doctor Jesus for the Worship of the Onion and a French-polisher, I chose the craftsman; I was thereupon adopted by his family, his colleagues and his favourite bistro – all that happened quite naturally, of course. That programme took up all my spare time.

Yet again I was forced to accept that as soon as my attitude starts to get logical, as soon as my timetable begins to run smoothly, the High Command sends someone to mess it all up again and make my research all the more chancy. And in view of what happened there was no danger of my falling into a systematic frigidity.

I met Robert Giraud at Romi's, a gallery in the rue de Seine where he was calmly waiting for a customer. In the daytime he was as somnolent as a cat, and he had much in common with that animal. But he didn't remind you of a nice pussy when you saw him like a furtive tom-cat on crepe soles, slinking close to the walls towards his nocturnal rendezvous. Sometimes – I found that a pity – he fought like a snarling tom-cat, ill-natured and mangy, but mostly he just lay in wait, leaning on a bar counter for hours, and as was to be expected there was always some vagrant of the night yearning for confidences who pushed his glass nearer.

He recounted these encounters to a class of Beaujolais-students at Fraysse's, the café and tobacco shop – I managed to get admitted too. It took the friendly pressure of this circle to get him to decide to write. The title of the book, *Le Vin des Rues*, was suggested by Jacques Prévert, who was immediately enchanted by the manuscript. It's a herbarium of 234 pages, in which can be found side by side nurses of love and their Julots, tramps and their tricks, assuring the survival of a threatened species, promoters of petty crime, and – not exactly the best people – some completely immoral vagrants; in short, a society which comes to the surface just as law-abiding citizens are slipping between the sheets.

One only had to follow Giraud; he moved around in that world relaxed and at his ease, like a fish in water. Only one regret slightly marred his bliss: that night vagrant, whom he had seen fleetingly in a bistro in the Halles, a lone wolf who had drained his glass and disappeared into the night – he had a death's head tattooed in his face. And despite all his energy, friend Giraud never saw him again. One could not hope to find a more committed supporter of revolt. With that big nose of his, did he scent the trail of new ideas? I don't remember, but anyway it introduced me to the world of tattooed people.

'Is there anyone with tattoos who wants to earn 200 francs?' You could hear that in *Aux cloches de Notre-Dame*, a bistro, now gone, on the corner of the rue Dante and the rue Laplace. They used to serve strong red wine in half-litre glasses – you had to keep your eye on your glass, or you might find it empty. No matter; the wine wasn't good, and personally I prefer it less rough.

Its clientele of tramps and ragmen were prime specimens. It was no problem if the tattoos were on the arm or the chest; the others were a bit more difficult. With Marceau, for example, it was a more delicate matter; his picture gallery was more spread out and had such a patina that it required a certain minimum of cleaning up. That permitted us to make the acquaintance of Melanie, in her digs, where she was frying two pickled herrings on a charcoal fire – on the walls were engravings from *Adam* magazine. She lamented: 'I wasn't expecting visitors, we're only ordinary workers – I'd have done the housework. You must have something to eat, just something simple. There'll be four of us, so go and get eight litres.'

The real masterpiece was Richardot, decorated from top to toe, a walking tapestry. A work of art doesn't have much connection with logic, but I always wondered what President Carnot was doing in that interlace of girls, animals and flowers. The only non-tattooed area was a triangle with its point downwards, covering eyes, nose and mouth. Under his underpants – Hell, of course.

The children used to hide under the bed when he came to the house.

Richardot came to a sticky end. He was appearing in bistros – 'For a few coppers I'll open my bath robe.' One fellow laughed, really poked fun at him. Richardot wasn't used to that: 'Step outside if you're a man.' The mocker went out first, a mistake. Richardot died in prison.

One more thing about him – on his identity card, under 'distinguishing marks', an official had entered 'None'.

In the archives of any newspaper or press agency there's always a box labelled 'Bizarre – fringe types – odd characters'. A junk-room in which tattooed people are found alongside collectors, enlightened fanatics and builders of castles in the air – all those with a horror of being classified.

Strangely, these builders of chimeras have one thing in common – there's always some voice which wakes them up, whether it's the Virgin Mary or one of their ancestors. It's always an order; there's no discussion, and hop! out of bed they get.

Like the others, Frédéric Séron obeyed the call from the other world, as could be seen from the menagerie of cement animals which had invaded his garden in Pressoir-Prompt along the Route Nationale 7.

I've never counted, but including the doves there must have been about a hundred inhabitants. In each animal was sealed a steel cylinder containing his visiting card, the local paper and sometimes the portrait of an official personage. That was his pyramid, his refusal to disappear completely. 'They'll find them a thousand years after I'm dead. I'm not afraid of death, but believe me or not, when I look at all that, it seems so vivid that I just have to go in the garden.'

A votre bonne santé! Frédéric Séron used to make his own wine; it was strong stuff, very highly coloured, but natural. Now the fashion's gone the other way. I've still got one of his pictures that he gave me, painted on plaster, an elephant hunt.

The coaches disgorge their tourists in front of the palace of the Cheval agency. The gentlemen of arts and letters are doing a Chartres tour, and with smiling condescension they deliver their patter, a bit of 'art brut' here, a bit of heritage there, in front of Raymond Isidore's mosaics made of broken plates.

Museum directors just love works created in the face of the mockery of their surroundings.

No one talks about Gilbert Frugier officially any more. Why? His case may be too specialised; one would have to open a new file with a resounding title such as 'collecting magician'. What motivated him was a love not only of collecting but of transforming.

I think I understand the recipe: take an object which has ceased to fulfil the purpose for which it was designed, and once it's separated from its purpose, like someone sent into retirement who devotes himself to some art, make it into an item of ornament or decoration. With its pillars made of stovepipes and chandeliers made of old light bulbs, his place felt like a palace of a thousand and one oddments.

The visit went on long into the night – the treasures filled two floors. I was dropping with fatigue, he was untiring. He appeared as Louis XIV with a wig of corks, disappeared behind a screen covered with post office calendars, whence he emerged as a knight in armour made of beer-bottle tops, rapidly replaced by the god Pan with horns made of teats that had been used to feed baby calves.

I thought I understood why his neighbours didn't appreciate him when he replaced his window shutters by panels representing grimacing Assyrian kings, which he'd found among the scenery of the theatre in Limoges. Harassing his neighbours or not, he was far too busy poking about in litter bins to spare them a glance.

The most important thing for armchair travellers is to get rid of the walls; Gilbert Frugier did that by covering them with things. There are other methods; personally I make no use of my ears but people tell me music brings good results.

Let's avoid debauched solutions and artificial paradises. Let's stay in the realm of precious materials – the veil of night seems to me a very effective protective cover.

First of all you have to learn to tame light, which is quite easy once the sun's gone down – at night you have the best chances of meeting those whom Jacques Yonnet calls the 'watchmakers of backwards time'.

The three colleagues I met after sunset did not come in the category of lovers of semi-darkness. As sports reporters they fitted better into the category of rubber gloves and new Beaujolais.

A stage in a bicycle race had brought us together for an evening in a thermal spa smothered in white wrought iron and globe lanterns. At the end of a dinner without mineral water we all agreed that it was bad for the health to go straight to bed after leaving the table, and anyway, any doctor'll tell you that. We strolled indolently out into the night with that typical walk of people taking the cure, who are going nowhere.

Nowhere be hanged – there must be a bistro on the route of the race, and there was, not a bistro but a bar, a luxury imitation with its inevitable American soldier boozing himself into a stupor and offering us Philip Morris cigarettes. The waitress floated around with that fixed sulky air which in those days was considered the ultimate in sex-appeal. Another girl stuck her head round the door every five minutes: 'Is Marcel here?' These two little things, spreading a sort of perfume of the underworld, quite naturally brought the conversation round to the subject of the disappearance of brothels.

And that was a sad story: 'Oh, the *Panier fleuri* – did you know the *As de Cœur* and the *Chasseur Magique*, with that girl from Martinique dressed in Alsatian national dress?' A few glasses of liqueur – raspberry and sloe, the kind that remind you of their presence the next day – sustained the climate of nostalgia. The closure of the closed houses is in itself an absurdity in the land of Descartes, but let that pass; the worst thing is that one will never again find that sort of baby-bliss, gurgling with pleasure and powdered with tender authority.

A new figure appeared at the wailing wall. I didn't see him join the group; he looked well-to-do, not exactly an old nobleman but not far off it. He didn't want to be indiscreet, but... (this'll amuse you!) 'I have my car outside, it's only five minutes away.'

We drove out of the town, a little Neuilly with villas, gravel, steps: 'I'll go up first, it's on the first floor.' A little steep staircase – 'After you, please.'

First of all you couldn't see much. When your eyes got used to the dark, the shock came: black stockings, bodices, suspenders – the ladies of the salon. Two were standing, looking as if they were talking; the rest of the 'staff' were scattered on three divans, leaving some free places for visitors. One woman was swinging her leg; the breast of another rose and fell; she was breathing – I was going to say 'still breathing'.

It was like a hallucination, a dusty nothingness, a kind of sickness. Our new friend was radiant: 'Do sit down, gentlemen, please, I'll put on some background music.' Well, complete with sighs, it was unbearable. A slushy horror.

Our colleague Louis, known as Loulou, found the appropriate words: 'It's very nice, but we mustn't be late, the start's tomorrow at seven o'clock...'

'We're awfully sorry; it was really very nice.'

He had done his best; in the car on the way back, no one opened his mouth.

'What are your deepest motives?' I'm often asked that. The formal way it's put doesn't fool me; what it means is 'Kindly explain your confounded mania for taking photos no one has ordered.'

An idiotic question; I haven't got a reasoned motive, only an irresistible urge to share the joy I have received through my eyes. It's purely instinctive. I keep all that to myself, but as I'm a polite person, I answer the aggressive question with a spoken pirouette: 'Refusal to disappear!' It's a front which neutralises the enquirer for a while and which is not entirely devoid of sincerity.

To disappear like in the cinema, to fade away at the end of the film, that's just about acceptable, but that brutal disappearance, click! – I can't conceive of it. For me, it's a reassuring picture to see the captain's hat floating on the water after the ship has sunk.

If all the busy collectors, all the pilers of stones that I've met had been asked the same question about motives etc., I wager they would have given similar replies. I sought their company in order to see how they set about disrupting the pendulum and slowing down time.

Once, and once only, I was too late. I found only a battlefield, a gutted house, statues on the ground, decapitated, mutilated, pitiful. The kids of Attigny hadn't waited long after the death of Camille Renault. A swarm of locusts. They too had speeded up erosion by playing with the pendulum.

Ghastly – poor man, he had taken such trouble to drape his figures, adding a piece of jewellery here, a fold there, perfecting, perfecting. In the middle of the carnage, I felt a twinge of the discomfort I felt in the war, on the day I found a doll in the ruins left by a bombing raid. Ghastly. The anguish of realising that posthumous works are a brake system without a guarantee is enough to discourage someone gifted with reason, and to sap his morale completely. In my case, as I said, it's only an instinct.

Light attracts me: a lamp goes on, I run like a madman – in insects that's called phototropism.

Boxing gloves and green peas

I haven't got the soul of a collector; I am not tormented by the desire to possess. Pictures are enough. I've lived in cohabitation with them for years. We know each other well, which allows me to say that pictures have their own characters and lives – perhaps they should be talked to, like plants, to make them flourish.

I haven't got that far, at least not yet; some of them are good little girls who give me a smile as I pass, while others are accursed trollops who never miss an opportunity to spoil things for me. I handle them with particular care.

Let's lower our voices a bit. In the gallery above the table at which I write there are three files, which in the course of years have become ever heavier; one day it'll take only one more picture, one of these unpleasant guests adding its weight to the load, to break the supports, and crash, bang! It would make a good item for the papers: 'Dramatic collapse!' But let's forget such embarrassing possibilities; what happens to me all the time is that I'm rummaging frantically in these files, someone's waiting on the phone, I've told them 'Just wait a minute!', a bit over-proud of my classification system.

A picture catches my attention and stops me dead; I'm caught as if in a bramble-bush, to such an extent that I completely lose track of what I was looking for. By the time I've extricated myself, the other person has hung up, probably furious to have rung me at all. Some people are funny like that; they don't seem to realise that some pictures in time acquire a kind of hypnotic power, while others become like elderly flirts, so out of date that meeting them again gives you a feeling of embarrassment.

You ask yourself: 'How could I produce a thing like that?' At the time I wasn't dissatisfied with myself, and actually it's quite well taken, nicely composed, quite original. Yes, but since then other photos have come along, a younger generation with more strident originality, whose brief triumph banished these pictures to the attic, although they too were only short-lived tricks. I'm satisfied with this explanation; mediocrity deserves no more, but I have no such easy explanation for the elixir of long life which some of my photographic companions seem to possess.

There's no recipe for it; that would be too simple, but all those pictures that grow old gracefully were taken using instinct, with total confidence in the intuition which brings much more than reasoning, and that's a good thing because you have to dare to be simple – that's so rare in an age full of intelligent people who know everything and see nothing. You often find an ingredient provided by the model, the look, this something, this heritage which you're not responsible for and which comes down to you from the depths of the ages. It twists around the optic axis and pierces photograph, celluloid, paper and spectator like a laser ray that broils everything in its path, including – and that's a very good thing – the critical sense.

Yes, I know, today you have to say 'Don't look at the camera!' That's an order, because the hunter must not be suspected of conspiracy with his prey.

Proud hunter, feather in his hat and nothing in his head. Looking aside means depriving the picture of the greater part of its mysterious power. That's how it is, I conclude; we must have the courage to report inexplicable things like the village idiot who brings back in his hat an egg of unknown species.

'Bizarre, I said bizarre, how strange it is'; I don't joke about such things any more, not since I met Pascal Fortuny. He lived alone in Montmorency, in a modest stone-built house whose interior, to say the least, was not exactly cluttered with useless coquetry. I took the portrait of a very old gentleman, bearded, more or less blind, wrapped in a dressing gown and wearing the beret of the mountain infantry.

His manner was one of distant benevolence; we passed the time in silence, since we didn't seem to have much to say to one another. When the time came for me to go, he suddenly became affectionate; he took my hand in his, which was long and like parchment. I also remember a ring with a very large stone, and then everything was empty, literally pumped out, white, a vacuum, and I was unable to drive the car.

Is there anyone in the room who can tell me what happened that day? No, get those gentlemen to sit down again; I didn't ask for two male nurses – a psychiatrist perhaps, or anyone who can express himself clearly. In this field it's probably like it is in the field of pictures; the words make nice music but don't get anywhere. It's less idiotic to keep one's mouth shut and let pictures speak.

If I talk of the magic power of a picture, draw in your claws, that's not what I'm talking about; the magic I'm talking about has nothing to do with the accessories of the bigger or smaller Albert. It may take on friendly forms, or it may come down on you like a ton of bricks when you're least expecting it.

It may for example come in the form of a letter – a new, distant friend you've never met has seen a photograph published in his daily paper at the other end of the world and conceived an irresistible desire to write to you. In such a case there must have been some phenomenon of harmonic vibration transmitted over a long distance without using the tangle of wires normally reserved for this purpose.

Or else I may find that magic on the ceiling of a lorry-driver's cabin on the Route Nationale 10, where I awoke in the early morning on the way to Couhé-Veyrac, welcomed by the smiles of a dozen Marilyns.

You have to surrender to that enchantment to enable it to become familiar; it's a field much less explored than researching a new mannerism, to which you intended to devote your youth. Leave that to the old; they have so few joys in life.

I cross the Pont Neuf in the company of the 'cultivated man'. To the west a shaft of sunlight bathes the Seine in sumptuous light. Just look! He grunts: 'A picture by Marquet.' As soon as a breach opens up and offers a view of the dazzling unexpected, he shovels it shut again with words. That's all that goes on inside him; he receives a piece of information in his head and at once he classifies it – anything but emotion, that factor of disorder and questioning, and anyway a bridge isn't the right place to admire things; there are museums for that, like other people say when they see lovers kissing in the street: 'There are hotels for that.'

I leave him to make his way to the Institute, bowed down by the weight of his erudition. Those types with their certainties are dangerous: if you let them, they'd stuff you alive. They're mere forensic scientists, legal-minded doctors who never helped anyone to live.

So that's that, bang! It's important to break a bit of porcelain from time to time, then you can tiptoe away, relieved and ready to start again.

There are days when the simple fact of seeing seems a real joy; you feel light as a feather – the police stop the traffic to let you pass. You feel so rich that you want to share your bursting joy with others. It's Sunday, as Prévert's plumber sings. The memory of those moments is the most precious thing I possess. Perhaps because they're so rare.

A hundredth of a second here, a hundredth of a second there, put together end to end; that never makes more than two or three seconds wrung from eternity.

Biography

1912 Robert Doisneau born on 14 April in Gentilly (Val-de-Marne).

1926 Admitted to the Ecole Estienne in Paris. Works in lithographic printing studio.

1929 Awarded engraver's diploma.

1930 Introduction to graphic design and commercial advertising photography.

1931 Becomes André Vigneau's camera-man.

1932 Sells first report to *L'Excelsior*.

1934 Starts career as industrial photographer at the Renault plant in Billancourt.

1939 Dismissed from Renault for repeated tardiness. Meets Charles Rado, founder of the Rapho agency, followed by first attempts at street photography. During general mobilisation called up as light infantryman.

1942 Meets Maximilien Vox who commissions him to illustrate a book, *Les Nouveaux Destins de l'intelligence française*.

1945 Starts work at the press agency Alliance Photo.

1946 Meets Raymond Grosset, then returns to the Rapho agency where he works with Blaise Cendrars, Jacques and Pierre Prévert. Begins collaboration with Pierre Betz, publisher of the review *Le Point*.

1947 Awarded the Kodak Prize.

1949 Signs contract with *Vogue* magazine.

1952 Does not prolong his contract with *Vogue*. Works with Robert Giraud on the theme 'Black stars, figures of the dark night'. Starts a new photo-musical symphony with Maurice Baquet, *Violoncelle-slalom*, which later becomes *Ballade pour violoncelle et chambre noire* published by Herscher in 1981.

1956 Robert Plécy awards him the Prix Niepce again.

1960 Sent by mistake to Palm Springs, California, to report on golf.

1968 Report on USSR for *La Vie Ouvrière* on 50 years of Soviet achievements.

1973 Produces a *court métrage* with François Porcile, *Le Paris de Robert Doisneau*.

1978 Participates in the film by Fernand Moscowicsz, *Trois jours, trois*

photographes, with Jeanloup Sieff and Bruno Barbey.

1979 His book *Le Mal de Paris* published by Arthaud, text by Clément Lépidis.

1981 François Porcile dedicates a film to him: *Poète et Piéton. Passages et Galeries du XIX*^e *siècle*, text by Bernard Delvaille, published by Balland.

1983 *Doisneau* by Jean-François Chevrier published by Belfond and *Robert Doisneau* in the 'Photo Poche' series published by the Centre national de la photographie. Participates in the shooting of a film by Bertrand Tavernier: *Un dimanche à la campagne*. Reprints of *La Banlieue de Paris* by Denöel, text by Blaise Cendrars, and of *Vin des rues,* text by Robert Giraud.

1984 Participates in the DATAR photographic mission on the theme: 'New urban landscapes'.

1986 Reprint of *Le Paris de Robert Doisneau et M. P. Fouchet* by Messidor. *Un certain Robert Doisneau* published by du Chêne. Balzac Prize.

1987 *Pour saluer Cendrars* published by Actes Sud and accompanied by an exhibition in Arles: 'Portraits of Blaise Cendrars'.

1988 *Doisneau* (Renault photographs) published by Hazan.

1989 *A l'imparfait de l'objectif* (memories) published by Belfond.

1991 Writer Daniel Pennac publishes a book on Robert Doisneau entitled *Les Grandes vacances*, which is based on his extensive collaboration with the photographer.

1992 A friend of Doisneau, actress Sabine Azéma, makes the fifty-minute-long film *Bonjour, monsieur Doisneau*. A conversation between Walter Benjamin and Robert Doisneau about Parisian passageways is published in the former's *Passages*. Is commissioned by his hometown, Gentilly, to re-photograph the motifs captured in his photographs of the 1930s and 1940s.

1993 Daniel Pennac publishes his second book on Doisneau, *La Vie de famille*. Patrick Cazals shoots two eighty-minute films for France 3, *Doisneau des villes* and *Doisneau des champs*.

1994 Robert Doisneau dies on 1 April.

Exhibitions

(A Selection)

Solo exhibitions

1951 The Fountain of the four seasons, Paris: 'The World of Spectacles'.

1960 Museum of Modern Art, Chicago (USA).

1968 Bibliothèque nationale, Paris.

1972 George Eastman Centre, Rochester Museum (USA).

1974 Galerie municipale du Château d'Eau, Toulouse, Vieille Charité, Marseilles.

1974 Witkin Gallery, New York (USA).

1975 Photogalerie Georges Bardawil, Paris. La Galerie et Fils, Brussels (Belgium). Musée des Arts décoratifs, Nantes. Musée Réattu, Arles. Galerie Neugebauer, Basle.

1976 Photo Art, Basle (Switzerland). Hôtel de Ville, Dieppe.

1977 Brussels (Belgium).

1978 Galerie Agathe Gaillard, Paris. Witkin Gallery, New York (USA). Musée Nicéphore Niepce, Chalon-sur-Saône.

1979 Musée Eugène Boudin, Honfleur. Musée d'Art moderne, Paris (June) and Tunis (November): 'The Passers-by Passing by'. Galerie du Château d'Eau, Toulouse: 'Robert Doisneau'.

1980 Amsterdam: 'Three Seconds of Eternity'.

1981 Witkin Gallery, New York (USA). Galerie Photogramme, Montreal (Canada): 'Robert Doisneau'.

1982 Fondation de la Photographie, Lyon, and French cultural services of the Embassy in New York: 'Portraits'. Town hall, Gentilly: 'Robert Doisneau: A Suburban Photographer'.

1983 From 1983 onwards, numerous exhibitions in France and abroad. Solo exhibition encompassing 120 photographs in Peking (China).

1984 Institut Lumière, Lyon: 'Sunday Photographer' (Photographs of the shooting of Bertrand Tavernier's film *Un dimanche à la campagne*). Since 1983, several exhibitions abroad, including the USA and China, and at the 'Maisons de la Culture' (Cultural Centres) in France.

1986 Crédit foncier de France, Paris: 'A Certain Robert Doisneau'.

1987 Musée de Saint-Denis: 'Saint-Denis'. Kyoto Museum (Japan).

1988 'A Certain Robert Doisneau' at the Villa Medici in Rome and the Institut français in Barcelona.

1989 Grande Halle de la Villette, Paris: 'Doisneau – Renault, 1934-1939'.

1990 Jardin des Plantes, Paris: 'Doisneau's Science'.

1992 Aberdeen Art Gallery, Oxford: 'Robert Doisneau: A Retrospective'. Since 1992, when the retrospective was opened by Doisneau, it has travelled to further venues, including Manchester (England, 1993); Lisbon (Portugal, 1993); Montreal (Canada, 1994); Paris (France, 1995); Kyoto (Japan, 1996); and Düsseldorf (Germany, 1997).

Group exhibitions

1947 Bibliothèque nationale, Paris: 'Photo Salon'.

1951 Museum of Modern Art, New York (USA) with Brassaï, Willy Ronis, Izis.

1965 Musée des Arts décoratifs de Paris: 'Six Photographers and Paris', with Daniel Frasnay, Jean Lattès, Jeanine Niepce, Roger Pic, Willy Ronis. Musée Réattu, Arles (France): exhibition with Henri Cartier-Bresson and André Vigneau.

1968 Musée Cantini, Marseilles (France): 'L'oeil objectif', with Denis Brilhat, Lucien Clergue and Jean-Pierre Sudre.

1972 French Embassy in Moscow with Edouard Boubat, Brassaï, Henri Cartier-Bresson, Izis and Ronis.

1975 Bibliothèque historique de la ville de Paris (France): 'Paris, la rue – Le Mobilier urbain'.

1977 Centre Georges Pompidou, Paris (France): 'Six Photographers in Search of Suburban Life', with Guy Le Querrec, Carlos Freire, Claude Raimond-Dityron, Bernard Descamps and Jean Lattès.

1983 French Association of Paris Architects, Paris (France): 'Les moins 30'.

Plates

1   The kiss in front of the Hôtel de Ville, 1950

2   The allotment, 1948

3   Place Pinel, 1975

4   At the gates of the Jardin du Luxembourg, 1953

5   Members of Saint-Médard parish, 1951

6   The accordionist, rue Mouffetard, 1951

7   The pure wool pullovers, 1933

8   Cherubims in the snow, 1978

9   Three little white children, 1971

10 Information, 1956

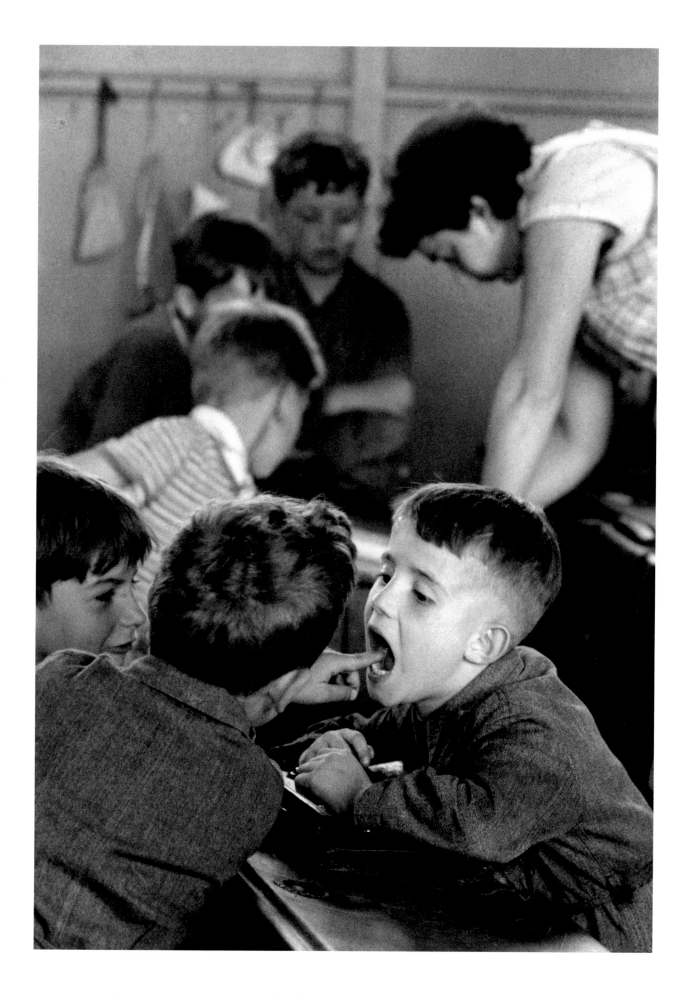

11 Practical exercises, 1956

12   Hell, 1952

13 Picasso's loaves, 1952

14 Suburban cinema-lovers, 1947

15   Cycle race in Gentilly, 1947

16   Wedding procession, 1949

17   The cats of Bercy, 1974

18   Sunday morning in Arcueil, 1945

19 Cement, tar and leisure, 1945

20 Aerial photography, 1950

21   The gyrating Wanda, 1953

22 The parents sitting outside, 1945

23   The inhabitants of the rue du Transvaal, 1953

24 Affectionate car-owners, 1960

25 The fearless one, 1952

26   Rue Robert Blache, 14 July 1951

27 The craftsmen's yard, 1953

28 The accordion of Kremlin-Bicêtre, 1932

29 Sunday artist, 1931

30 Fox terrier on the Pont des Arts, 1953

31   A Sunday stroll, 1933

32 A sideways glimpse, 1948

33   A balcony seat, 1953

34 Coffee and cream, 1948

35 The bistro as a world of its own, 1950

36   Standing at the bar, 1954

37 The four seasons – spring, 1960

38   Angels and leaks, 1953

39 The fallen horse, 1942

40   The gentlemen of the Quintaine, 1952

41 The mimosa, 1952

42 Coco, 1952

43 The giants of the north, 1951

44 The collector Gilbert Frugier, 1951

45 Two bellies on 14 July 1955

46 Fine Thursdays off school, 1957

47 The kids of Place Hébert, 1957

48   In the gardens of Vert Galant, 1950

49   A bench in the Palais-Royal, 1950

50   The sinking car, 1944

51　The doorbell, 1934

52 Dog on wheels, 1977

53   The brothers, 1937

54 Fishing with a dry fly, 1951

55 Concours Lépine, the unsinkable boat, 1954

56   Diono the dog trainer, 1946

57   The Salkazanof children, 1950

58   The little kids with the milk, 1932

59 The Cour Carrée at the Louvre, 1969

60 Jacques Prévert on the Pont de Crimée, 1955

61 Grappling with Venus, 1964

62   The Langeais fire brigade, 1977

63 The unveiling, 1964

64   The office of the *Aile droite* in Roubaix, 1951

65 Shooting it out, 1953

66   The bride's ribbon, 1951

67   Passers-by in the station square at Ivry, 1949

68   Bathers in La Varenne, 1945

69   The ladies of the Bois de Boulogne, 1953

70 A cycle ride in the springtime, 1948

71 The oasis of the Ile Saint-Louis, 1949

72   Dad's airplane, 1934

73   Place du Tertre, 1956

74   Mum and Dad's house, 1955

75 Maurice Baquet and his chamber music, 1957

76   A couple from the Quai de la Rapée, 1951

77 The fleeced calf, 1968

78　Once there was a worker at the Peugeot works who wanted to sabotage the steel shafts,1952

79   Traffic jam in the Rue des Petits-Champs, 1969

80   Saul Steinberg's bath tub, 1955

81　Dream girls, 1952

82   Maurice Arnoux, Marcel Riffard, Louis Caudron, Coupe Deutsch, 1937

83   Jean Marais, Jean Cocteau, 1949

84   Comtesse Gaëlle d'Oncieu de Chassardon and Monsieur Pedro Corcuera, Biarritz, 1950

85 Elsa Maxwell's tittle-tattle, 1950

86   The white horse, 1972

87   Versailles, captive barbarian and the Callipygian Venus, 1966

88 A glimpse behind the stage with most sincere compliments, 1952

89 Les Halles metro station, 1945

90 The music-mad butchers, 1953

91 The last waltz of 14 July 1949

92   The changing room at the Central, 1954

93 The standard rose, 1946

94   Mademoiselle Anita, 1951

95   The pack, 1969

96 The helicopters, 1972

97 Enagg gymnasium, 1947

98   Intimate friends only, 1945

99 The bride at Gégène's, 1946

100 The higher animals, 1954

101 Monsieur Barré's Roundabout, 1955